I am...

l am her

With special thanks to:

Jason Aldrich, Gerry Baird, Jay Baird, Neil Beaton, Josie Bissett, Laura Boro, Melissa Carlson, Tiffany Parente Connors, Jim & Alyssa Darragh & Family, Rob Estes, Pamela Farrington, Michael & Leianne Flynn & Family, Sarah Forster, Michael J. Hedge, Liz Heinlein & Family, Renee & Brad Holmes, Jennifer Hurwitz, Heidi Jones, Sheila Kamuda, Michelle Kim, Carol Anne Kennedy, June Martin, David Miller, Carin Moore, Moose, Jessica Phoenix & Tom DesLongchamp, Steve & Janet Potter & Family, Joanna Price, Jose Rodriguez & Kittens, Diane Roger, Alie Satterlee, Kirsten & Garrett Sessions, Andrea Summers, Brien Thompson, Helen Tsao, Anne Whiting, Kobi & Heidi Yamada & Family, Justi and Tote Yamada & Family, Bob and Val Yamada, Kaz & Kristin Yamada & Family, Tai & Joy Yamada, Anne Zadra, August & Arline Zadra, Dan Zadra, and Gus & Rosie Zadra.

Credits

Written by: M.H. Clark;
Designed by: Heidi E. Rodriguez.
Color Photography by:
Yevette Inufio and Beth Retro.
Black and white photography is vintage.

Dedications

To my mother, who lives the most beautiful example, and to Ang, Becca, and Maitreya. {M.H. Clark}

To my mother, a constant light, and to my sister, who always leads the way. {Heidi E. Rodriguez}

Who is she?

She is a daughter. *She* is a best friend. She is a pocketful of light. She is a spark of something good, getting brighter; a dream grown large; the right thing at the right time.

She is a dancer, a singer, a thinker, a truth-teller. A connoisseur of all the things this wide world has to offer. Her spirit is the first thing people notice. Her mind always had a mind of its own. Her heart, though it has sometimes been hurt, bears a strong resemblance to a daffodil: it always flowers again.

So *she* wakes with anticipation. *She* finds new hills to climb. And everyone agrees that the very fact of her in the world means there is still so much good to come.

Who is *she*? *She* is me. *She* is you.

I am her.

"As a woman
I have no country.
As a woman,
my country is the
whole
world."

Virginia Woolf

JUN · 58

She needs no map to discover where she is going, or how to get there. Her map is written on her heart—its roads and rivers are her dreams, her strength, her confidence. The way is not always easy, but when she takes a moment to notice the scenery, she sees that it is always beautiful.

I am her.

She soaked in the light

turned a new corner

The branches above her,

the shadows at her feet,

and stepped off the sidewalk

into bloom.

heard her song,

and gave it room.

Enjoy yourself.

"This day
is a journey,
this
very moment an
adventure."

Rebecca Pavlenko

She promises herself adventure, new places, different views, a chance to get lost. She infuses her day with newness and wonder. She brings a camera everywhere, notices the little things, gets a cup of coffee at a different cafe, takes the long way home. She discovers so much unexpected joy. She begins to love the journey.

I am her.

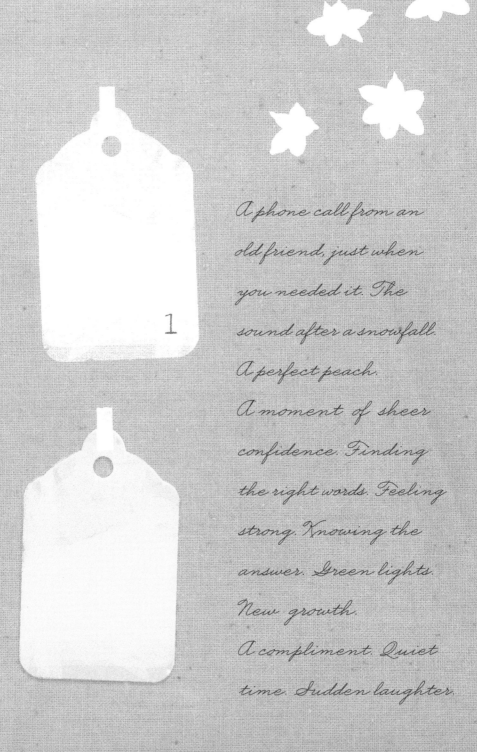

1

A phone call from an old friend, just when you needed it. The sound after a snowfall. A perfect peach. A moment of sheer confidence. Finding the right words. Feeling strong. Knowing the answer. Green lights. New growth. A compliment. Quiet time. Sudden laughter.

2

3

4

"The future belongs to those who believe in the beauty of their dreams."

Eleanor Roosevelt

She still speaks to the little girl
who wanted to be an artist, a doctor,
a poet, a wing-walker. She listens
when that little girl talks, when she
paints pictures of the clouds, when
she draws something huge in sidewalk
chalk. She makes her every day a place
for old dreams and new dreams, dreams
that tower and dreams that whisper.

I am her.

"Knowing what you want is the first step toward getting it."

Mae West

WISHES I'VE MADE:

WISHES I HAVEN'T
EVEN ADMITTED YET:

WISHES I WILL MAKE:

Live *big*

"Your playing small
does not serve the world.
There is nothing
enlightened
about shrinking so that other people
won't feel insecure around you.
We are all meant to
shine, as children do."

Marianne Williamson

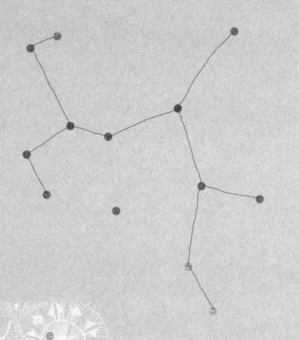

She unfurls her wings. She speaks her mind.
She is a beautiful parcel of boldness and grace,
all wrapped together, brilliant. Shining.
The more of her own light she allows to shine,
the more others shine too. From high up, she
imagines they must look like a constellation.

I am her.

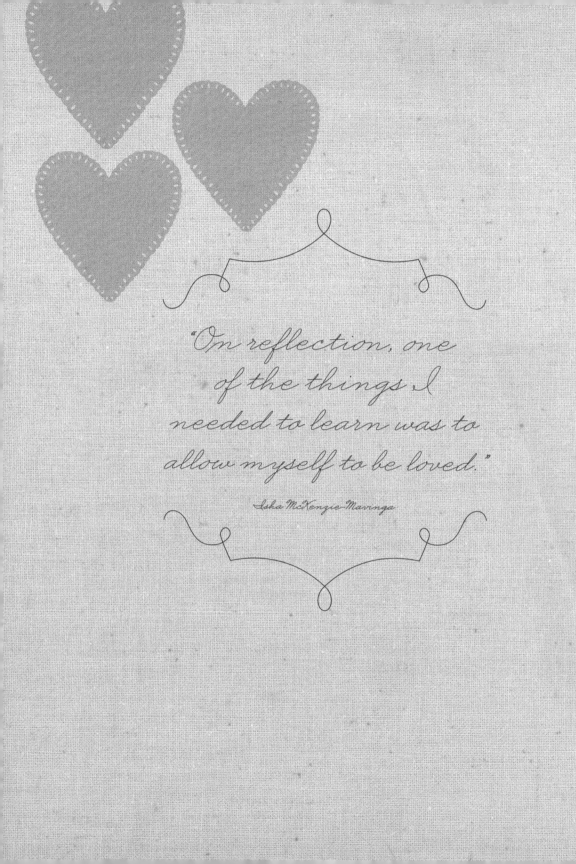

"On reflection, one of the things I needed to learn was to allow myself to be loved."

Isha McKenzie-Mavinga

Write all the nice things people say about you. Choose at least one to believe every day.

COMPLIMENT PRACTICE!

Turn

your

light

on.

Shine the fact of it out into the world.

Watch what happens next.

"Self-respect has
nothing to do with the
approval of others."

Joan Didion

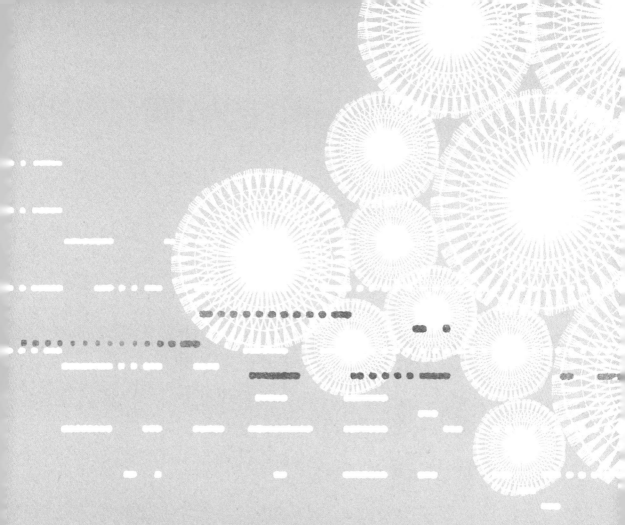

She wants to be beautiful, wants a flash,
a spark, a rare and wonderful spirit
that everyone sees. But before all of
that, she wants to respect herself.
As is. Even the shaky parts. Because
even the shaky parts have a shine to
them that doesn't fade. She grows ever
stronger in the life she has made.

I am her.

Love your *extraordinary* self.

Turn away from the
world this year and
begin to listen. Listen
to the whispers of your
heart. Look within.

Sarah Ban Breathnach

SHE WON'T:

She lies awake and listens to what her heart has to say, hears it declare that this is the beginning of her own new year, and in this year

SHE WILL:

AND SHE'LL START:

"I read and walked for miles at night along the beach...searching endlessly for someone wonderful who would step out of the darkness and change my life. It never crossed my mind that that person could be me."

Anna Quindlen

"It is only the first step
that is difficult."

Marie de Vichy-Chamrond

There are some days, some tasks
that seem like hills to climb.
Lately, she does not mind them
so much. She finds that once
she begins them, she has more
momentum than she had imagined.
The muscles of her legs and
the muscles of her mind begin
to crave worthy challenges.

I am her.

"Change doesn't happen in the middle. It only happens when we venture over to the edge and take one small step after another."

Karen Sheridan

THE REASONS:

THE MAP:

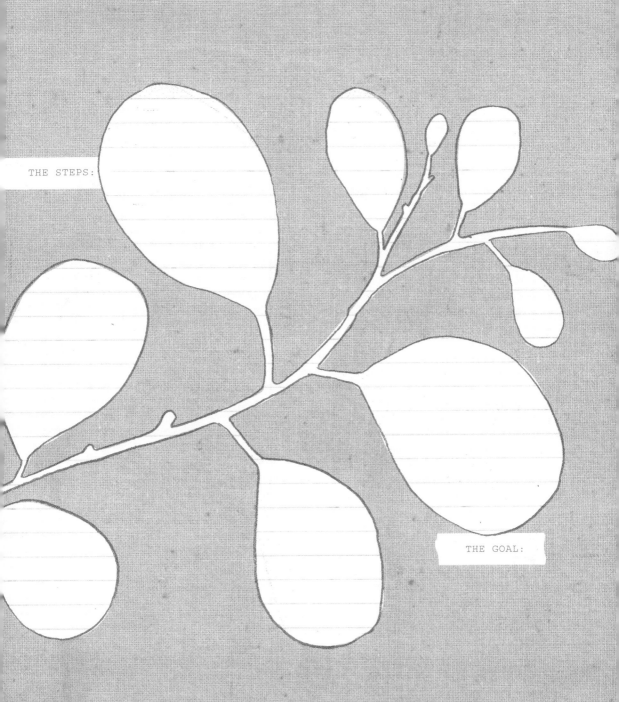

THE STEPS:

THE GOAL:

"Until we see what we are,
we cannot take steps to
become what we should be."

Charlotte P. Gilman

"I am not afraid. I was born to do this."

Joan of Arc

She puts on the shoes that make her stand
tall, buttons her buttons, sees herself in
the mirror: resilient and beautiful and ready.
There is nothing in this day that is too much
for her. There is nothing she cannot meet with
clear eyes and a willing heart and a strength
that bubbles up inside her like a spring.

I am her.

"See every difficulty as a challenge, a stepping stone, and never be defeated by anything or anyone.

Eileen Caddy

"I need to take an *emotional* breath, step back, and remind myself who's actually *in charge* of my life."

Judith M. Knowlton

I give myself permission to:

⟡⟡⟡⟡⟡⟡⟡⟡⟡⟡⟡⟡⟡⟡⟡⟡⟡⟡⟡⟡⟡⟡⟡⟡⟡⟡⟡⟡⟡⟡⟡⟡⟡⟡⟡⟡

⟡⟡⟡⟡⟡⟡⟡⟡⟡⟡⟡⟡⟡⟡⟡⟡⟡⟡⟡⟡⟡⟡⟡⟡⟡⟡⟡⟡⟡⟡⟡⟡⟡⟡⟡⟡

⟡⟡⟡⟡⟡⟡⟡⟡⟡⟡⟡⟡⟡⟡⟡⟡⟡⟡⟡⟡⟡⟡⟡⟡⟡⟡⟡⟡⟡⟡⟡⟡⟡⟡⟡⟡

⟡⟡⟡⟡⟡⟡⟡⟡⟡⟡⟡⟡⟡⟡⟡⟡⟡⟡⟡⟡⟡⟡⟡⟡⟡⟡⟡⟡⟡⟡⟡⟡⟡⟡⟡⟡

⟡⟡⟡⟡⟡⟡⟡⟡⟡⟡⟡⟡⟡⟡⟡⟡⟡⟡⟡⟡⟡⟡⟡⟡⟡⟡⟡⟡⟡⟡⟡⟡⟡⟡⟡⟡

STARTING THIS VERY MOMENT.

Write your own permission slip for the field trip
you've been needing, the dream you've been holding,
the thoughts you haven't allowed yourself to voice.

Give yourself permission to *live.*

"If you don't like the way the world is, you change it. You have an obligation to change it. You just do it one step at a time."

Marian Wright Edelman

She doesn't do so well at standing still.
She plans big, she rolls up her sleeves,
she has faith in her own momentum. She
knows that change doesn't happen all at
once, but she welcomes it, she prepares
for it, she gives it fertile ground.

I am her.

"You gain strength, courage, and confidence by every experience in which you really stop to look fear in the face...You must do the thing you think you cannot do."

Eleanor Roosevelt

THINGS THAT ARE
TRUE ALREADY:

THINGS TO
MAKE TRUE:

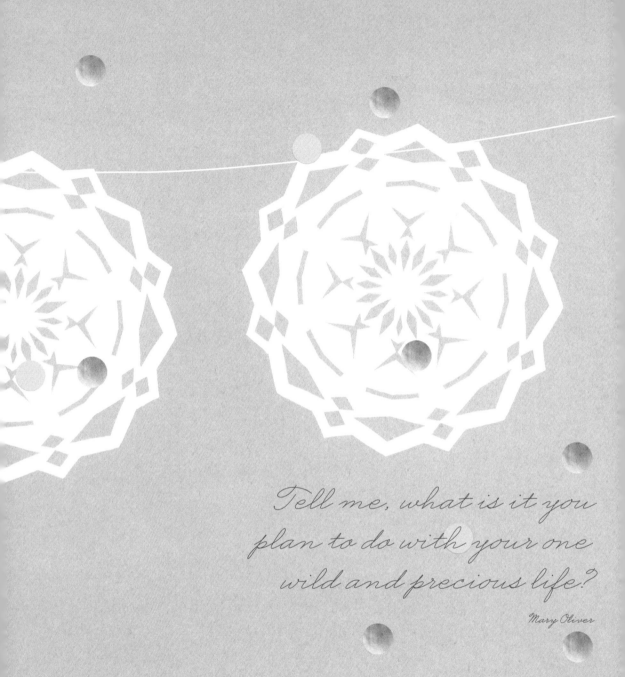

Tell me, what is it you plan to do with your one wild and precious life?

Mary Oliver

She has her plans: design a building, run
with the bulls, camp in the Arctic, fly a
plane, learn a new language, open a pastry
shop, learn to dance the conga beautifully
(in red heels). She wants to learn how to
live and how to love and how to hold her own
in this world that is so wide and wonderful.

I am her.

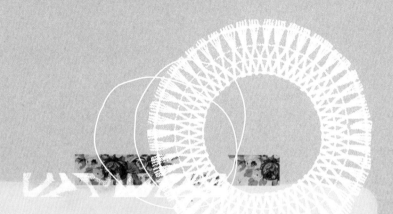

250

"I'm not a has-been. I'm a will-be."

Lauren Bacall

AND I WILL BE:
(CIRCLE ALL THAT APPLY)

Adaptable/Adventurous/Affectionate/Articulate/
Artistic/Assertive/Balanced/Brave/Brilliant/
Buoyant/Calm/Clearheaded/Comfortable/
Committed/Compassionate/Competitive/
Confident/Conscious/Considerate/Content/
Cooperative/Courageous/Creative/Curious/
Decisive/Determined/Eager/Elegant/Energetic/
Enthusiastic/Excited/Fantastic/Flexible/Focused/
Forgiving/Fulfilled/Generous/Graceful/Grateful/
Grounded/Gorgeous/Happy/Hard-working/
Honest/Imaginative/Independent/Influential/
Innovative/Insightful/Inspired/Involved/Joyful/
Kind/Loving/Loyal/Motivated/Natural/Open-minded/
Organized/Original/Passionate/Patient/Positive/
Productive/Receptive/Reliable/Responsible/Secure/
Self-aware/Shining/Sparkling/Stable/Strong/
Tenacious/Unflappable/Visionary/Willful

"I will not die an unlived life. I will not live
in fear of falling or catching fire. I choose to
inhabit my days, to allow living to open me, to
make me less afraid, more accessible; to loosen
my heart until it becomes a wing, a torch,
a promise. I choose to risk my significance,
to live so that which came to me as seed
goes to the next as blossom, and that which
came to me as blossom, goes on as fruit."

Dawna Markova

Do what you *love*.

"Female friendships that work are relationships in which women help each other belong to themselves."

Louise Bernikow

32

She keeps the dreams her friends forget.
The ones that seem to be too big or too
distant, or built for someone else. And
when the moment is right, she returns them
to their owners, reminds them what they've
always known: step by step, the stars are
reached. Our friends help do the climbing.

I am her.

"The most beautiful people we have known are those who have known defeat, known suffering, known struggle, known loss, and have found their way out of the depths. These persons have an appreciation, a sensitivity, and an understanding of life that fills them with compassion, gentleness, and a deep loving concern Beautiful people do not just happen."

Elisabeth Kübler-Ross

168

work

o'clock!

"*There is time for work, and time for love. That leaves no other time.*"

Coco Chanel

250

love

o'clock!

Time for:

Time for:

love

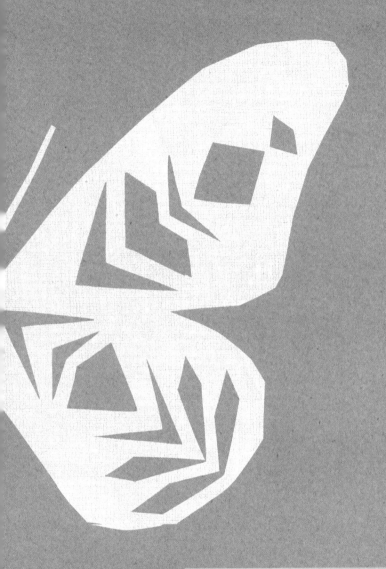

"It is never too late to be what you might have been."

George Eliot

" *All the women* I know *feel* a little like *outlaws.* "

Marilyn French

They stay out late, they call each other at unexpected times, they give each other's crazy ideas a place to grow. They make their own rules, and then they break them. They push the envelope, they wear big boots, they grab onto the things they want and never let them go.

I am her.

"I was always looking outside myself for strength and confidence, but it comes from within. It is there all the time."

Anna Freud

" *Earth*
is crammed
with heaven. "

Elizabeth Barrett Browning

She gets goosebumps from tiny, perfect things.
Seeing the stars. Fruit trees in bloom. The
scent of dinner from a neighbor's house, a
phone call at the right time, a bar of exotic
chocolate. She keeps a list in her wallet of the
gorgeous parts of the everyday: maple leaves,
new perfume, slow-cooked tomato sauce. She adds
to it all the time. She is rich with wonder.

I am her.

Today is a good day to welcome
the unexpected, celebrate the way
its plans unfold.

Today is a good day to pack a small bag,
cross a new border,
send a picture postcard to the future.

Listen to the *true, wise, knowing* statements of your heart.

THINGS TO REMEMBER:

THINGS TO CREATE:

be her.